HONEY FROM
THE HONEYCOMB

HONEY FROM THE HONEYCOMB

SWEET ARE THE WORDS
SPOKEN BY GOD

TADD WEBBER
WITH
MILLARD OWENS

iUniverse, Inc.
Bloomington

HONEY FROM THE HONEYCOMB
Sweet Are the Words Spoken by God

iUniverse books may be ordered through booksellers or by contacting:

iUniverse
1663 Liberty Drive
Bloomington, IN 47403
www.iuniverse.com
1-800-Authors (1-800-288-4677)

ISBN: 978-1-4759-4784-7 (sc)
ISBN: 978-1-4759-4785-4 (hc)
ISBN: 978-1-4759-4786-1 (ebk)

Library of Congress Control Number: 2012916125

Printed in the United States of America

iUniverse rev. date: 08/31/2012

Biblical citations are from the New American Standard Bible (NASB), King James Version (KJV), and New King James Version (NKJV).

INTRODUCTION

In Psalm 19:7-10, (NKJV) the Holy Scriptures state the following:

The law of the Lord is perfect, converting the soul; the testimony of the Lord is sure, making wise the simple; the statutes of the Lord are right, rejoicing the heart, the commandment of the Lord is pure, enlightening the eyes; the fear of the Lord is clean, enduring forever; the judgments of the Lord are true and righteous altogether. More to be desired are they than gold, yea, than much fine gold; sweeter also than honey and the honeycomb.

When God opened the Scriptures to me and the Holy Spirit revealed its meaning, it was sweeter than honey from the honeycomb.

In July 1949, I was gloriously born anew, and my life has never been the same. After my salvation experience, I looked for someone to teach me how to walk and act before God. I could not find anyone to tell or show me.

I went to the One who did have answers because I felt that God deserved more honor, praise, and worship than I knew how to give. I searched the Scriptures and found that a person has to die to come alive in Christ. As I studied the Scriptures, questions came alive in me, and again I asked the Lord to give me answers.

I lived in the Middle East for seventeen months, working in the Sahara Desert. There, I saw things I had never seen before. I realized that the Western mind does not have a clear concept of God and His Word. I will endeavor to cover some of these topics in this book.

The goal of this book is to open people's eyes to the hidden nuggets of knowledge that are so often overlooked in the Scriptures. As examples, I will describe my personal experiences to the reader. I will use His Holy Word to examine how God answers prayers and ensures that various individuals can develop His plan for mankind.

Tadd Webber

CHAPTER 1

As I noted in the introduction, I spent seventeen months working in the Sahara Desert. It was there, as I traveled from one site to another, that the answers to some of the questions that were lingering in my mind were revealed.

One of my primary questions was, how a vineyard can be planted in a rocky and arid land, which in bible days, was the case. I knew, from my studies of the scriptures, that they must have planted several vineyards, since the use of grapes for wine had been mentioned numerous times. In John 2:1-10 (NKJV), Jesus was at a wedding feast and they ran out of wine. The scripture states that Jesus' mother instructed one of the servants, "You do whatever He tells you to do". He told them to bring six water pots which had been filled with water for the purification of the Jews. Each of these pots could hold from twenty to thirty gallons. After the servants filled the water pots with water, He then said, "Draw out some and take to the master of the feast". The master of the feast was amazed at the quality of the wine and questioned the bridegroom why he had held back the good wine. I realized that wine was used for numerous things. Some of the scriptures that mention wine and its uses are Lev. 23:13, offerings, Gen. 27:25, drink, Esth. 1:7, festive drink, Luke 10:34, disinfectant, Mark 15:23, drug, and 1 Tim. 5:23, medicine.

In my travels, I came upon a grape vineyard. The plants were placed in a hole that was approximately two feet deep. This protected them from the sun's tremendous heat, in the morning and the evening. The vine received enough sun through the noon period to heat the hole and allow any condensation from the cool night air to collect around the plant. The grapevine was about the size of a man's upper arm and had little branches that covered the fruit.

Now you might wonder why this would be important to Christians today. Let's refer to the Holy Scriptures, specifically John 15:1 in which Jesus says, "I am the true vine, and my Father is the vinedresser." In verse 5, He goes on to explain that we are the branches, and all we need to do is cover the fruit that He causes to be produced.

My second question had to do with sheep and the shepherd. In John 10:1-16, we are told that Jesus is the good shepherd; His sheep will hear and respond to his voice because they know His voice and will not follow any other.

I had the opportunity to see a sheepfold in the desert. The fence surrounding it was approximately twelve feet wide and eight to ten feet tall. The only entrance into the sheepfold was an opening large enough for the sheep and goats to enter. A man could not stand upright to enter but would have to crawl through. The fence was not a wire or wooden structure as we have in the states. Cactus had been planted around the pen in which sheep and goats were to be kept. Sand would blow in and cover the cactus that had been planted and this process had been allowed to take its natural course for years.

When evening came, the night guard would allow each shepherd to drive his herd into the sheepfold. The herds consisted of both sheep and goats. The night guard would then lie in the hole and protect the herds. The only way a robber could gain access into the fold was to climb the cactus wall or drag the night guard out of the hole. When morning came, the shepherds reappeared. Each one issued forth a different sound, and his herd would hear and make their way to him. I could not tell for sure how many sheep and goats were in each herd but I would estimate in access of twenty.

In John 10:9, Jesus tells His disciples, "I am the door, and anyone who enters by me will be saved, and will go in and out and find pasture." Oh, how important it is for us to hear the voice of our Shepherd and follow, not adhering to any voice other than His. Do we always know our Shepherd's voice, and do we always follow that voice?

After seeing the grapevines, something that I'd wondered about for a number of years suddenly became clear: a phrase from the Song of Solomon 2:15(KJV): "It's the little foxes that spoil the vine." When I flew back home from the desert, the first thing I saw was a little pup chewing anything he could get his teeth on. Then I understood the phrase. A little fox was like the pup, chewing on anything to ease the pain of new teeth coming through. With those new teeth he could damage the grapevine and cause it to die.

Here in the story about the grape vineyard, it is important to know that the same type of fence that was around the sheepfold also surrounded the vineyard. The only thing that could scale the fence was the fox.

These are but a few of the things that were revealed to me. God the Father is faithful to His children. He feeds the hungry and satisfies those who are thirsty.

I found it hard to have a clear understanding of the Holy Scriptures as long as I tried to discern it with my Western mind. I consider it a blessing of God to have lived and worked in the Middle East and to see the terrain so close to where Jesus walked.

CHAPTER 2

G enesis 11:27-31 begins the story of Abram. He was the son of Terah, who was a descendant of Shem, one of the sons of Noah. Abram married Sarai, who was a very beautiful woman, but she was barren and did not bear any children.

Genesis 12:1-20 describes how the Lord God spoke to Abram and directed him to leave the land of his birth and travel to a land of the Lord's choosing. Abram departed as the Lord had spoken, taking Sarai and Lot, his brother's son, along with all their possessions. They went to Canaan, a land of promise. Abram passed through the land and went to Shechem, where he built an altar at the site of a giant oak tree. God told Abram that He would give this land to Abram's descendants.

The Scriptures mention other great trees that are associated with great men. In Judges 6 through 7, (NKJV), we are told that an angel of the Lord sat under a terebinth tree in the city of Ophrah. Once again the people of Israel had sinned and were being tormented by their invaders . . . They cried to God because of the cruelty they were enduring. God sent His angel to the area where Gideon was threshing wheat for his father Joash, of the tribe of Judah. The angel told Gideon, "The Lord is with you, you mighty man of valor!" God spoke directly to Gideon and told him to go in this strength to deliver Israel, which he did.

Genesis 35:4 relates that Jacob told his household to give him all of their idols and earrings, and he buried them under a terebinth tree in Shechem. When Deborah, Rebekah's nurse, died, she was buried under a terebinth tree, Genesis 35:8. In the Bible, the terebinth tree is described as a landmark, a burial place, and in Isaiah 1, a place of judgment. The ancient Hebrews did not do anything that did not have meaning or purpose.

In the book of Joshua, the Bible relates that Joshua, a military leader, entered, conquered, and then occupied the land, as was promised by God. Joshua 23:11-16 states plainly that all good things will come to those who love God. Furthermore, those who do not honor God or His covenant soon learn that His anger will burn against them, and they will perish quickly. In Joshua 24, God renews His covenant with the Hebrew children. In verses 27 to 28, He undertakes the long task of dividing the Promised Land among the twelve tribes. At the end of this division, God does as he has promised. The people take possession of the land, and God delivers their enemies into their hands.

Abram continued to move on to the mountain east of Bethel and pitched a tent with Bethel on the west and Ai on the east. The distance between these two towns is approximately five miles. He built an altar to the Lord and called His name.

As Abram continued his journey south, there was a severe famine in the land. Therefore, he decided to travel down to Egypt. At this time, Abram began a line of deceit that would continue throughout his family for generations. He told Sarai if she was questioned by the Egyptians about her relationship to him, she should tell them she was his sister. This very thing happened, and Pharaoh took her because of her beauty. Pharaoh treated Abram well for her sake, and because of this Abram became very rich. He had livestock, silver, and gold when He departed from Egypt. However, the Lord God spoke to the Pharaoh and informed him of Abram's deceitful act. Pharaoh called Abram to him and asked why he had done this, and Abram told him he was afraid the other men would lust after Sarah and would kill him to get her.

Sarai had not given any children to Abram, so she devised a plan to provide him with a son. She gave her handmaiden, Hagar, to him as a wife in the hope that she would bear him a son. Hagar, when she saw that she had conceived, despised Sarai. Abram told Sarai that she could do to her handmaiden as she pleased. Sarai began to treat

Hagar harshly, and Hagar fled from Sarai's presence and went into the wilderness. There, an angel from the Lord appeared to her and told her to return to her mistress. When Abram was eighty-six years old, Hagar bore him a son, and Abram called him Ishmael, which means God hears.

As we look further into the accounts about Abram, we find that God told him to have a blameless, upright walk before Him. God also told Abram that He would make a covenant with him and that Abram's descendants would multiply and he would be the father of many nations. This was the covenant of circumcision. God told Abram that it would be an everlasting covenant for him and all his descendants. At this time, God also changed Abram's name to Abraham, which means "father of many nations." God also said that Sarai would be called Sarah and that He would bless her, and she would also give Abraham a son in a year. God said that this son would be named Isaac, which means laughter, because both Sarah and Abraham laughed at the thought of having children at their advanced ages.

Abraham's journeys led him to the south, and he lived between Kadesh and Shur and stayed in Gerar. Abimelech was the king of Gerar. Again Abraham said that Sarah was his sister, and because of Sarah's beauty, the king took her. God came to Abimelech in a night dream and told the king that Sarah was another man's wife. Abimelech had sinned by taking her, and as a result he was a dead man. Abimelech had not gone near her, and he asked God if He would slay a righteous nation because he had been deceived. Abraham had been deceptive and said that Sarah was his sister. Sarah had agreed with her husband and said that Abraham was her brother.

God told him to restore the man's wife, for he was a prophet who would pray for the king, who would live. Abimelech took sheep, oxen, and male and female servants and gave them to Abraham and restored his wife to him. This seed of deceit planted by Abraham would be inherited by many subsequent generations.

God visited Sarah and opened her womb. Abraham was approximately one hundred years old and Sarah was ninety when she bore Abraham a son. Isaac was Abraham's son of promise. When Abraham had grown very old, Isaac came to the age where he could choose a wife. Abraham called his oldest servant, who ruled over all that he had. Abraham instructed the servant to swear that he would not allow Isaac to marry a woman from Canaan. Instead, the servant was to go back to Abraham's homeland and choose one of the daughters of the land for Isaac. The servant took ten of his master's camels, departed, and made his way to the city called Hamor in Mesopotamia. He prayed to the Lord God and asked that God give him success and show kindness to his master, Abraham. He asked if, as a way of confirming he'd chosen the right lady, he should say to her, "Please let down your pitcher that I may drink." Then she would say, "Drink, and I will also give your camels to drink."

As he was speaking, Rebekah, the daughter of Bethuel, a son of the wife of Abraham's brother, came out with her pitcher on her shoulder. She was very beautiful, and as she came toward him, he asked for a drink from her pitcher. She lowered her pitcher and gave him a drink. Then she said, "I will draw water for your camels also." The servant told Laban, Rebekah's brother, all the things that had come to pass because of his oath to Abraham. Laban then gave Rebekah to the servant as Isaac's wife. After Rebekah's approval of the arrangement, they blessed her, and she and her maids departed with Abraham's servant.

Isaac had gone out in the field to meditate when he saw the camels approaching. When she saw Isaac and was told who he was, Rebekah dismounted and covered herself with a veil. The servant told Isaac all things that had happened. Isaac was forty years old when he took Rebekah as his wife.

As Isaac's mother was barren, so also was Rebekah, and she did not bear him children. He pleaded with God on her behalf, and God granted his plea. She became with child, and within her womb there were twins. They struggled in her womb, and she asked the Lord why this was so. The

Lord told her that there were two nations in her womb, and two peoples would be separated from her womb. One people would be much stronger than the other.

Isaac was sixty years old when the twins were born. The first twin was hairy all over, and as a result, he was called Esau. The second was named Jacob, which means supplanter or deceitful. Esau was a skillful hunter, but Jacob was a mild-mannered man. Isaac loved Esau because he ate his son's game, but Rebekah loved Jacob.

One day, Esau went out in the field to hunt, and when he returned, he was weary and extremely hungry. Jacob had prepared a pot of lentils, and Esau begged him for the stew. Jacob said if Esau sold his birthright, as the firstborn, to him, he could have the stew to eat. The birthright of the firstborn son was that, when his father died, he would inherit a twice as much of his father's possessions as his siblings did. Esau said that since he was about to die, he had no use for the birthright anyway. He sold it to Jacob for a serving of the stew. Esau's name then became Edom meaning red, which was the color of the stew.

Another famine, similar to the one Abraham had experienced, came upon the land. Isaac moved to Gerar, where Abimelech was king. Isaac devised in his heart a deception to tell the men of that place that Rebekah was his sister, because she was so beautiful. He feared for his life if the men desired her.

After Isaac lived in Gerar for a long time, Abimelech saw Isaac showing endearment to Rebekah, and he knew that Isaac had deceived the men of the country. Abimelech called Isaac to him and told him that he knew of the deceit. Abimelech charged all the people not to touch Isaac or Rebekah, and anyone who disobeyed would be put to death.

Now the time had come when Isaac was old, and his eyes were dim. He called his eldest son, Esau, to him. Isaac said to Esau, "Behold, I am old and do not know the date of my death. So take your bow and quiver, and go out into the field and hunt game for me. Make me tasty food, such as I love, and bring it to me that I might bless you before I die."

Rebekah heard Isaac's words, and while Esau was in the field, she devised a plan to deceive her husband into giving his blessing to Jacob. Rebekah said to Jacob, "Go to the flock and bring two of the best goat kids. I will make a tasty meal for your father, such as he loves. You will then take it to your father so that he will bless you before he dies." Jacob said to his mother, "My brother is a hairy man, and I have a smooth skin. My father might feel me and know that it is not Esau, and I shall bring a curse upon me." Rebekah then said to him, "Let your curse be upon me, my son, but obey my voice and do as I have directed you." Jacob did as his mother had told him, and she cooked the meal.

She went and got Esau's best clothes. She took the skins from the kids and put them on Jacob's arms and hands so that he might seem to be his brother. Jacob took the food to his father and continued the deception by telling Isaac, "I am your son, Esau." His father requested he come closer so he could feel him. Jacob did so, and when Isaac asked again if he were Esau, he said once more, "Yes, I am." At Isaac's request, Jacob went and kissed his father. His father smelled him, and because of the clothing he was wearing, he did smell like Esau. Isaac then pronounced his blessing upon Jacob. When Esau discovered his brother's deceit, he was very angry and hated Jacob. Rebekah told Jacob to go to her brother's house and stay there until Esau's wrath had subsided.

Genesis 28-35 offers an account of Jacob's life. He went to the house of his mother's father in Padan Aram. He was instructed to choose a wife from the daughters of Laban, his mother's brother. Laban had two daughters, Leah, the oldest, and Rachel, the younger.

Jacob chose Rachel to wed, and he agreed to work for her father for a period of seven years as dowry for her. After the seven-year period, the deceitful Laban brought his eldest daughter, Leah, to Jacob's wedding bed, and he went into her. In that land, the tradition was that the younger daughter should not be allowed to marry before the eldest.

Laban asked Jacob to fulfill the customary wedding week with Leah, and then if he agreed to work another seven years, Laban would then give him Rachel, to wed. Jacob agreed to this and continued to work for an additional seven years. After this period of time, Rachel was given to Jacob to wed.

Rachel was Jacob's favorite wife but she was barren. Leah conceived and bore him six sons.

Rachel gave her maid to Jacob, and she bore him two sons. Leah gave her maid to Jacob, and she bore him two sons. This now gave Jacob ten sons and yet his favorite wife still remained barren.

God then remembered Rachel and she became pregnant and gave birth to Joseph, which means he will add. Jacob loved Joseph very much and favored him over all of his other sons.

When Jacob's period of service had been completed, Laban asked Jacob to stay and continue working for him. Jacob agreed to stay, on the condition that he receive all of Laban's spotted, speckled, and brown lambs. Laban agreed to Jacob's demands.

But after a time, Laban became very unhappy with the agreement because he saw that God blessed Jacob with a great number of the sheep that were spotted or speckled.

He said to Jacob, "From this date all the sheep that are born speckled or spotted shall be added to my flocks." Under this new arrangement, Jacob would get the plain sheep. God blessed Jacob once more, and his flock was increased as greatly as it had been under the previous agreement.

The sons of Laban said, "Jacob has taken away all that was our father's and has gathered much wealth." We do well to remember that everyone will not be overjoyed with our blessings from God. Laban became angry because of the wealth that Jacob had gained, and his countenance began to reveal that displeasure. Jacob heard the words that were spoken against him. And when he saw Laban's face, he realized that he no longer had the favor of his father-in-law.

The Lord spoke to Jacob and told him to return to the land of his father. Jacob took his family and all of his possessions that he had gained from his father-in-law, and he started on his journey to return to his father's land.

After three days, Laban heard about Jacob's departure. He then pursued him for seven days. Laban overtook Jacob at a place where he had pitched his tents in the mountains and asked why his daughters and their children had been taken away before he had a chance to kiss them and tell them good-bye. Jacob said, "I was fearful that you would take your daughters away from me by force."

Then Laban accused Jacob of further evil doings. He asked, "Jacob, why have you also stolen my gods and idols?" Because he was not guilty of doing this thing, Jacob answered, "With whomever you find your gods, you may take his life."

Laban went into all the tents and searched, leaving Rachel's tent until last. Rachel had taken the household idols and had hidden them in the camel's saddle and sat on them. She said to her father, "Let it not displease you that I cannot rise before you but the manner of women is upon me." So Laban did not find them.

Jacob was angry with Laban, and he told the men with him to take stones and make a heap as a way to separate him from Laban. God had blessed Jacob, and he returned to his father's land a very wealthy man. Laban intended his deceitfulness to increase his own wealth and not Jacob's, but God meant to bless Jacob.

Jacob sent messengers to Esau, his brother, and commanded them to tell him, "I have been in the land of Laban these many years and have returned with much wealth. These servants were sent ahead to tell you, my lord, that I pray I might find favor with you."

Jacob's messengers returned to him and said, "Your brother Esau is coming to meet you with four hundred men. This report made Jacob fear that his brother might be coming for revenge. He divided the people into two camps along with his herds and flocks. He thought that if his brother came and attacked one camp, the other could escape.

Jacob began to talk to God and said, "God of my fathers, Abraham and Isaac, who told me to return to the land of my father, deliver me. I pray that you will deliver me from the hand of my brother, Esau."

Jacob lodged there that night. When morning came, he took two hundred female goats, twenty male goats, two hundred female sheep, twenty male sheep, thirty milk camels with their colts, forty cows, ten bulls, and twenty female donkeys with ten foals. He delivered these into the hands of his servants and said, "When Esau meets you and wants to know to whom you belong and where you are going, tell him that you are my servants and that all these are sent by me, his brother, as a gift to him and that I am coming behind you. Tell him that I hope this gift will please him, and afterward, when I see his face, perhaps he will accept me." The present and his servants went on before him but he lodged that night in the camp.

Jacob was left alone, and a man wrestled with him all night long, until the break of day. Now when the man saw that he did not prevail against Jacob, he struck the socket of Jacob's hip, and it went out of joint. He said to Jacob, "Let me go, for the day breaks." Jacob said, "I will not let you go until you bless me." The man then asked, "What is your name?" Jacob replied, "My name is Jacob." The man said, "Thy name shall be called no more Jacob, but Israel; for as a prince has thou power with God and with men, and has prevailed". (Genesis 32:28). (KJV) This man was Yashua, the Christ, Jesus, and he was sent to Jacob as his savior or deliverer. A detailed search of the Scriptures reveals the many things that Jacob did because of his feelings of guilt toward Esau. He devised many means of repaying Esau for the wrong he had done to him by stealing his birthright. He forgot, as so many do today, that God changed his name from Jacob, which means deceiver, to Israel, which means God strives.

When we become children of God, we should no longer allow ourselves to be controlled by fear. Yashua, Jesus, the Savior and Deliverer, was sent so that we can walk in the newness of life. We do not have to walk in our works of flesh, because God will fight our battles for us. The renaming of Jacob as Israel by God is one more confirmation that he had a higher calling, and that he would no longer walk alone but God would always be with him. Jacob walked with a limp from that time on. There is a possibility that his limp saved his life when he first met his brother. Because of the limp, Esau might have taken pity upon him and become reluctant to cause any harm.

Jacob saw Esau coming with four hundred men. He then did as he had planned: he divided his men; he crossed over to Esau's men, and bowed himself to the ground seven times as he came near to his brother. Esau ran to meet him and embraced him, and they were reunited.

Some might assume that, because of the size of Esau's army, he planned to destroy Jacob and all that was his. This would have been in recompense for the wrong his brother had done to him. After many years of study of Hebrew customs, in my opinion, there would have been no honor for Esau if he killed or destroyed a lame man. Therefore, he did not attack Jacob or his camp.

CHAPTER 3

Jacob journeyed to Succoth, where he built houses for the people and shelters for the livestock. Then he went to the city of Shechem, which is in the land of Canaan, and pitched his tent on a parcel of land that he bought from the children of Hamor.

Jacob and Leah had a daughter whose name was Dinah. One day, Dinah went to see the daughters of the land. Shechem, the son of Hamor, saw her, took her, lay with her, and had relations with her, thus defiling her.

A modern Western mind would probably think of Shechem as a no-good individual who took advantage of a young lady. But according to eastern culture, a chaste young lady would never have gone out alone without an escort. Since Dinah had done so, Shechem thought she was a woman of low esteem. Shechem realized his mistake when she bled as a virgin, and he knew he had taken a woman of pure virtue.

The Middle Eastern mentality concerning the family and women is as follows: All family members are raised to know and have pride in the ancestry of the family and tribe, even if they are dirt poor. The father will train the oldest son from an early age in the family business and his father's trade. In some family cultures, the sons pay one-quarter of their earnings to the father for their entire lives. These funds are intended to take care of the parents in their old age. The more sons there are, the better the finances of the father; fewer sons mean fewer finances.

The woman is raised to be chaste, discreet, and a good wife; to love, take care of, and be obedient to her husband; to be a good homemaker, and to love her children, training them up in the way they should go. In the New Testament, the older women are told to teach the younger women in these ways, so that the word of God may not be blasphemed. This is found in Titus 2:3-5, and is more proof that God does not change his mind from one time period to another. As the Scriptures state in Numbers 23:19, "God is not a man that He should lie; neither the son of man that He should repent; hath He said, and shall he not do it? Or hath He spoken, and shall He not make it good". As I read this it conveys to me that His Word is yea, amen, or so be it.

When a man becomes interested in a young woman, the head of his tribe or family will go to the father of the young lady and negotiate a price or dowry so that she may become his wife. A well-taught young lady may bring a high price. A man might be forty-two years old before he can save the money to attain a wife. After the wedding night and consummation of the union, the bed sheet will be displayed to attest that the bride is a virgin.

If a father has a number of daughters and barters well for them, as Laban did with Jacob, he can become rich, which could also qualify him to sit at the gates of the city as a judge.

The prayer of Jabez, because it gave most Christians insight into how much God cares for His children caused quite a stir. Scriptures state that Jabez was more honorable than his brethren (1 Chronicles 4:9-10). Had God used any others like him? The only other one mentioned in the Scriptures is Shechem. Genesis 34:19 states that Shechem was more honorable than anyone in his father's house. Genesis 34:1-31 relates the story of Shechem, son of Hamor the Hivite, a prince of the country, and Jacob's daughter.

As stated previously in this chapter, Shechem had defiled Dinah, and now his soul was attracted to her, and he realized that he loved her. He also knew that he had to right the wrong he had committed. It was the custom that his father, Hamor, would request the hand of the young lady from her family. Shechem went to his father and told him of his desire to wed this young woman and thus correct his misdeed. Hamor decided in his heart to make an agreement with Jacob.

Jacob heard that Shechem had defiled his daughter, Dinah, but he held his peace until his sons returned from the fields, where they had been tending the family's livestock. When they heard about their sister's defilement, the sons of Jacob were grieved and angry. They considered Shechem's act a very disgraceful thing.

Hamor spoke to Jacob and his sons. "My son Shechem longs for your daughter," he said. "I pray that you would grant his request and give her as his wife. Then you can make marriages with us by giving your daughters as wives, and we will give our daughters to be your wives. You shall dwell with us, and the land shall be available to you for trading and to acquire possessions."

Shechem then spoke to Dinah's father and her brothers: "Please let me find grace in your eyes and in what you shall require of me, I will give. Ask of me so much dowry and gifts and I will give according to what you shall say unto me, but give the damsel to me as my wife."

The sons of Jacob answered Shechem deceitfully, because he had defiled their sister. They said to him, "We cannot give our sister to one who is uncircumcised, for that is a reproach to us. We will consent unto this marriage if you will become as we are, and every male among you is circumcised. Then we will give our daughters to be your wives, and we will take your daughters as our wives. We will dwell with you, and we will become as one people; but if you will not agree to be circumcised, we will take our daughters and be gone."

Their words pleased Hamor and Shechem. The young man and his father agreed to the terms because the young man had delight in Jacob's daughter, Dinah, and he was more honorable than all the house of his father. Therefore; they did not want to delay to do the thing that the household of Jacob demanded.

Hamor and Shechem went to the gate of their city and said to their men, "These men are at peace with us. Therefore, let them dwell in the land and trade in it. This land is large enough for both households. It shall be that we will take their daughters as our wives and give our daughters as their wives. The only way that this can be accomplished is for us to agree to their conditions, that is, every man among us should be circumcised as they are. If this thing is accomplished, will not their livestock, their property, and every animal of theirs be ours? So let us consent to them, and they will dwell with us."

On the third day after the men were circumcised, and they were in a great deal of pain, two of Jacob's sons, Levi and Simeon, took up their swords and killed them all. Then they slew Hamor and Shechem with the edges of their swords and took Dinah from their house.

Jacob's sons slaughtered the men and plundered the city because of the defilement of their sister, Dinah. They took all the sheep, oxen, and donkeys, all that was in the city and their fields. They then took all of their families into captivity after plundering their houses.

Jacob was very distressed with Simeon and Levi. He told them that they had made a stench among all the inhabitants of the land, the Canaanites and the Perizzites. He reminded them that since they were few in number, the people of Hamor's land could gather themselves together and destroy his entire household. But they said, "Should we allow our sister, Dinah, to be treated as a harlot?"

God told Jacob, "Arise and go into the land of Bethel, which means house of God, and dwell there. Make there an altar to God who appeared to you when you fled from the face of your brother, Esau." Jacob said to his family, "Put away any foreign gods that you have among you, purify yourselves, and change your clothing. We shall then arise and go to Bethel so that I follow the commandments of God. This I shall do because He answered me in the day of my distress."

They gave all of their strange gods and idols and the earrings from their ears to Jacob, and he hid them under the terebinth or oak tree in the city of Shechem. Approximately twenty years later, they would arrive in Egypt, where they were held captive for another four hundred thirty years. Then God sent Moses to bring them out. They wandered in the wilderness, for an additional forty years, before they were allowed to enter the Promised Land again.

After the land was divided up between the twelve tribes of Israel, Joshua took the Ten Commandments back to the tree in Shechem. Even though neither Shechem nor his tribe was saved, his nation was.

Once we are aware of the events that occurred among the nations and tribes of Israel, we should realize that the next five hundred years could be affected by the actions that take place today.

The terror of God was on all the cities around, and the inhabitants did not attack or pursue Jacob and his family. So Jacob and all who were with him went to Bethel or Luz, which is in the land of Canaan. They built an altar there and called it El Bethel; because it was there that God appeared to Jacob when he had fled from his brother.

And God appeared unto Jacob, when he came out of Padan Aram and blessed him. And God then said unto him, "Thy name is Jacob, thy name shall not be called any more Jacob, but Israel shall be thy name and he called his name Israel." This time, He continued, "I am God Almighty, be fruitful and multiply, a nation and a company of nations, shall be of thee, and kings shall come out of thy loins. And the land which I gave Abraham and Isaac, to thee I will give it, and to thy seed after thee will I give the land. ". And God went up from him in the place where He talked with him. Genesis 35:9-13. (KJV)

As we continue to study the Scriptures, we find that each time God does a great work in a man; He changes his name, as he did with Abram, changing his name to Abraham. He did likewise to Jacob, changing his name to Israel, and Saul of Tarsus, changing his name to Paul, before he confronted the magician Bar-Jesus (Acts 13:6-13).

Israel set up a pillar of stone in the place and poured a drink offering upon it. And he did as God had instructed him and called the place Bethel or a place of God.

As the company continued to travel, Rachel bore a son she called Ben Oni, which means son of my sorrow. His father, Israel called the boy Benjamin, which means son of my right hand. Rachel died after this childbirth and was buried. Israel set up a stone that was called the pillar of Rachel's grave. After this, he traveled further and pitched his tent beyond the tower of Eder.

Isaac, Israel and Esau's father, was one hundred and eighty years old, when he breathed his last and died. Israel and Esau buried him.

CHAPTER 4

Genesis 37 relates the story of Jacob's favorite son, Joseph. Jacob's other sons, whose mothers were Leah and the two maids, were very jealous of the love that he showered upon Joseph. Jacob made him a coat of many colors and when his older brothers saw it, they hated him and could not even speak to him peaceably.

Joseph had two dreams. In the first dream, Joseph saw himself and his ten brothers in a field and they were all binding sheaves. He saw his sheave stand up and the other sheaves bow to his. In the second dream, the sun, moon, and eleven stars bowed down to him. He told his father and brothers about these dreams. His father admonished him, "Shall your mother and I, as well as all your brothers, bow down to the earth in front of you?" His father kept these matters in his heart, but his brothers hated him.

One day, Jacob sent Joseph into the fields where his brothers were feeding the sheep. He told his son to see if his brothers and the flock were okay and to bring back word to him. When Joseph arrived where they were supposed to be, he did not find them. A man told him they had left to go to Dothan, so he followed and found them there. Dothan is an ancient city located fifty-five to sixty miles north to northwest of Jerusalem. The brothers saw him coming and began to devise a plan to kill him. They planned to deceive their father and say that a wild beast had killed Joseph. They said, "We shall then see what becomes of his dreams." Reuben, Joseph's oldest brother, thought he might in some way save the boy's life and deliver him back to their father. He said, "No, let us not shed his blood but throw him into the pit in the wilderness."

They took Joseph's coat of many colors and cast him into the pit. A band of Ishmaelite's came by, and the brothers conspired to sell Joseph so they could profit from him and still not shed his blood. They spread blood from the kid of a goat on Joseph's coat of many colors and took it to their father. They did indeed deceive their father, telling him that a wild beast had killed his favorite son. Jacob could not be comforted after the loss of Joseph.

The Ishmaelites took Joseph to Egypt and sold him to Potiphar, a high-ranking Egyptian officer and captain of Pharaoh's guard. You can read about Joseph's life in Egypt in Genesis 38-41. Eventually, he became known as an interpreter of dreams, and news of this reached Pharaoh, who sent for him.

Joseph interpreted two of Pharaoh's dreams to mean that there would be a great famine in seven years, but before that Egypt would have an abundance of food. Pharaoh put Joseph in charge of storing the food, to prepare for the time of famine. Just as Joseph had predicted, after seven years, there was a great famine over the face of the earth. When the Egyptian people became famished, they cried to Pharaoh, who told them to go to Joseph and to do all that he told them. Joseph opened the storehouses and fed the people of Egypt.

All the other countries went to Egypt to purchase grain. When Jacob saw that there was plenty in Egypt, he sent all of his sons, with the exception of his youngest, Benjamin, to purchase grain. The sons of Jacob came before Joseph but did not recognize him. Joseph knew his brothers but he acted like they were strangers. He accused them of being spies who had come to see the nakedness of Egypt. They said, "No, we are but sons of one man, Israel. We are honest men and mean no harm. Ten of the sons of Israel are here now. The youngest is still at home, and one of us is dead and is no more."

After hearing their story, Joseph said, "You shall not leave this place until one of you returns home and brings the youngest brother to me. The rest of you shall be imprisoned until this brother is presented to me." They would not agree to this, and so they were all imprisoned for three days. After the third day, Joseph sent for the brothers and told them that he would allow all but one brother to go and take the grain to their father. If they returned with their younger brother, the other would be released.

The consciences of the brothers began to accuse them of the wrong they had done to their brother Joseph. They were sure that God was now repaying them for this act.

Joseph understood all that they were saying but did not make himself known. He turned away from them and wept.

He took Simeon and bound him before them. Joseph commanded his servants to fill the brothers' sacks both with grain and the money they'd paid for that grain. One of the brothers discovered his money when he went to feed his animal, and they were all very afraid.

The brothers went to their father and told him all things that had happened to them. Jacob declared that he would not allow his youngest son to be taken since he was the only one of Rachel's sons left.

After a certain period of time, the family used all of the food that had been obtained in Egypt. Jacob told his sons to take a present to the man in Egypt. They were to take double the money as well as their youngest brother. They did as they were told and traveled to Egypt and stood before Joseph.

When Joseph saw that they had brought Benjamin, he instructed the steward to take them to his house and prepare a feast to be eaten at noon. The brothers were afraid because they were being taken into Joseph's house. They thought that he would demand some recompense for the money that they found in their sacks during their first return home.

When Joseph came home, the brothers presented the gift that had been sent by their father. Joseph inquired into their father's welfare and was told that he was alive and well. The brothers bowed down to the earth, prostrating themselves before him. When he saw his younger brother, Joseph was overcome, and he went into his chamber and wept. He arose, washed his face, and went back to his brothers.

After they had eaten, Joseph directed his steward to fill their sacks with food and to place his silver cup in Benjamin's sack. The steward did as he was instructed and then sent them on their way. Silver denoted wealth and authority and the cup could have been a gift from Pharaoh to Joseph in return for interpreting his dreams.

When the brothers had departed the city but had not yet gone very far, Joseph sent his steward to catch up to them. He instructed him to ask why they had repaid good with evil. He was to say to them, "My master's silver cup, from which he drinks, has been taken." He did as his master had instructed. When Joseph's brothers were accused, they said:

> Why do you accuse us? Do you not remember that we returned with all of the money that we found in our sacks of grain? Does this speak of our honesty and integrity? With whomever you find the silver cup, let him die and we will return to your master and become his slaves.

The steward began his search. He started with the oldest brother and ended with the youngest. When he opened Benjamin's sack, the silver cup was discovered. All the older brothers were wrought with grief but they loaded the donkeys and returned to the city as they had promised they would.

When Joseph saw the sincerity of his brothers, he could not restrain himself any longer. He told everyone to leave so that he would be alone with his brothers. He began to weep so loud; all the Egyptians and the house of Pharaoh heard it. Joseph told his brothers to come close to him. He said:

> I am Joseph, your brother, whom you sold into Egypt. But now, do not be grieved or angry with yourselves, because God sent me before you to

preserve your lives. So now consider this fact that it was not you who sent me here, but God. God has made me a ruler throughout all of Egypt. Now return to our father and tell him of all these things.

When Pharaoh heard the report that Joseph's brothers had come, he told Joseph, "Tell your brothers to return home, pack all that belongs to your father and his family, and then leave the land of Canaan. I will see to it that they have the best land in Egypt, and you will eat of the fat of the land." Joseph sent his brothers back to their father. He instructed them to return home and to bring their father and all of the family back to Egypt, which they did.

The heart of forgiveness comes from God only when we are obedient to His word. The curse of the brothers' deception has been carried through the generations, but it has now been brought to light. The result of their deception was approximately 430 years of bondage and slavery in Egypt.

After their father's death, the brothers thought within their hearts that Joseph might hate them for the thing that they had done to him. They hurried to Joseph and asked for his forgiveness, which he readily gave. In Matthew 6:14-15, we are instructed that if we forgive men their trespasses against us, our heavenly Father will also forgive our sins. If we don't forgive, then our Father will not forgive us.

This is a very important thing we can learn from this incident of Joseph. He was without total peace until he openly forgave his brothers.

CHAPTER 5

The children of Israel were in bondage in Egypt for 432 years. They had increased in number from the original seventy descendants of Jacob, but all those who had originally come into the land, including Joseph, had died. All of the descendants of the seventy had been fruitful and multiplied, and they grew exceedingly mighty.

A new Egyptian king, who had not known Joseph, came into power, and he was sorely afraid of the Israeli people. He said to his people, "The children of Israel are more and mightier than we are. If we go to battle with our enemies and the Israelites join them and fight against us, we will surely be forced out of our land."

Taskmasters were set over the children of Israel, but the more they were afflicted, the more they multiplied and grew.

The Egyptian king called all of the Hebrew midwives before him and instructed them to kill any male child born to a Hebrew woman. The midwives feared God and did not follow the king's instructions. When the king called them back, they said, "Hebrew women are unlike Egyptian women. They give birth before midwives are called."

The decree then went out that all male Hebrew children who were two years old and younger were to be killed. We learn this in Matthew 1:16.

One boy was saved by being placed in a basket that was put to float in the reeds along the river's bank. The daughter of Pharaoh came to the river to bathe and found the baby, whose sister had stayed by the river to see what the fate of her brother was to be. She went to Pharaoh's daughter and asked if she could find a Hebrew woman who could nurse the baby for her. Pharaoh's daughter told her to do so.

The sister called for her mother, who went to Pharaoh's daughter. The boy child's name was Moses, which means "drawn out." Moses was raised in the Pharaoh's house as a son of Pharaoh's daughter. He was the one chosen by God to bring His people out of their bondage in Egypt.

To fully understand God's call to Moses to do this monumental task, read the entire book of Exodus. There, you will also read about the testing of Pharaoh's heart, the plagues, the four hundred years of bondage, and the harsh treatment withstood by the Hebrew nation. Exodus describes the wilderness trip and the disobedience of God's children.

The people endured hardship at the hands of their masters. A way of escape from sins committed during the year was provided by laws (Leviticus 16:1-34). The Day of Atonement was established and observed once a year. On that day, the blood of an innocent animal was offered as a substitute for sin committed that year. This Day of Atonement was always on the tenth day of the seventh month of the Jewish calendar.

There had to be sacrificial blood offerings to atone for uncleanness in the priesthood, the tabernacle, and the nation. These Levitical laws were established to effect mind-and-heart changes in the Hebrew children who had been freed from Egypt.

In accordance with Hebrews 9:11-28, a new covenant was established and ratified. This covenant was satisfied by the sacrifice of the Perfect Lamb, the Lord Jesus Christ. Included under this covenant are all who believe in the Son of God and accept Him as their Lord and Savior. Hebrews 9:28 states, "Christ was offered once to bear the sins of many." Romans 5:8-10 tell us that Christians have been given freedom and life by the death of the Son of God, Jesus." After Moses led the Hebrew children for forty years, God told him that it was time to step aside. Moses asked God to select the man who would succeed him, and Joshua was chosen.

After Moses died, God told Joshua:

> My servant Moses is dead. You rise and go over
> the Jordan, with the children of Israel, to the land
> that I have given them. Every piece of land upon
> which you put the soles of your feet shall be yours.
> I will never leave you nor forsake you. Be strong
> and very courageous that you may observe all my
> laws as Moses commanded of you. Do not turn to
> the left or the right that you may prosper wherever
> you may go.

Joshua was accepted by the children of Israel, who told
him, "All that you command us to do we will do. Wherever
you tell us to go, we will go. Let anyone who will not heed
your words and obey you, be put to death."

Joshua then sent two men into the land to secretly
check it out. Joshua requested that they look especially
at Jericho. They went to Jericho and came to the house
of Rahab, where they stayed. The king of Jericho heard
about them, and he sent one of his men to Rahab and
asked if two Hebrew men had indeed stayed in her house.
He commanded that she should send them out if they were
there. Rahab took the two spies upon the roof and hid
them in stalks of flax. She told the king's emissary that
two men had come to her house but she did not know

from where or what they had come to do. Rahab and her family had heard about the things that God had done for the Hebrew children, and they believed. The two spies told her that when God delivered Jericho into their hands they would deal kindly with her and her family. She was advised to hang a red string from her window, and when the war ensued she and her family would be saved.

The men returned to the camp of Joshua and told him about their journey and all that happened. They told him that surely the Lord had given Jericho into their hands because the people there were fainthearted.

God told Joshua how to cross the River Jordan with the children of Israel, on their way to the Promised Land. Joshua was to send the priests bearing the Ark of the Covenant before the men of war. When the feet of the priests stepped into the river, the waters would stack up, and the people could then walk across on dry land and continue to journey to the Promised Land. The crossing of the Jordan happened exactly as God said it would. God's words are yea and amen, and He is not a man that He should lie.

Twelve men, one from each tribe, were selected to choose one stone from the shore to take across the Jordan. The men placed the stones on the banks of the river as a memorial, so people would know exactly where they crossed.

As the Hebrews approached Jericho, they found the city gates tightly closed due to the inhabitant's fear of the Israelites. God told Joshua that He was giving him this land of Jericho as well as its king and all of its mighty men. God instructed Joshua to take seven of the priests and give each one a trumpet made from a ram's horn. Followed by the mighty men of war, the priests were to make one trip around the walls of Jericho for each of the next six days without any sound. On the seventh day, they were to march around the city seven times, this time shouting and blowing their trumpets.

They did so, and the walls of the city fell flat. They went in and destroyed all that was in the city. This happened because of the Lord's promise to Joshua and the people of Israel. When God makes a promise to His children, He always delivers.

Joshua instructed the two men who had spied on the land to retrieve Rahab, the woman who had hidden them from the king. They had promised that she and her family would not be harmed in any way. The two spies went in before the battle and took Rahab, her father, her mother, her brothers, and all that she had to the Israelites' camp. (This is the same Rahab who is included in the genealogy of Christ.)

The city of Jericho—all of the inhabitants and their goods—were burned after the capture. The children of

Israel were instructed to not take any of the city's things lest they become cursed as well. All of the silver, gold, and the vessels of bronze and iron were to be consecrated to the Lord and taken into treasury of the Lord. The children of Israel did not listen. They took the things into their camp. And the anger of the Lord burned against them.

Joshua sent spies to survey the country of Ai. They were to report on the number of men of war and the strength of the country. The spies returned and reported that there was no need to send all of the men of Israel into battle against Ai. When the men of Israel went into the city, the men of Ai came upon them and slew thirty-six men. The men of Israel fled, and their hearts melted and became like water.

Joshua fell on his face before the Ark of the Covenant and stayed there until evening. He and the elders of Israel lay there and put dust on their heads. Joshua could not understand why such a defeat had happened at Ai. He questioned God about why He had taken them so far and then delivered them into the hands of their enemies. (Since Ai was considered to be a small city why is scripture referring to enemies in the plural. Were the citizens of Ai called Amorites? In doing further research, I went to maps of ancient cities. Maps of the area show that from 2000-1400 BC, the Amorites controlled an area from the Arnon River Valley, the border on the south and Mt.

Hermon on the north. The city of Ai was in this area. There were several cities located in the Amorite territory, with Ai being the smallest. They had become a laughing stock of all the inhabitants of the land.

God spoke to Joshua. "Get up! Israel has sinned in that they did not honor my commands. They took some of the cursed things in Jericho and put them among their own stuff. The children of Israel could not stand before their enemies because a curse has come upon them, and they have become doomed to destruction. It shall be so until the cursed things are removed from among you."

Achan, a man from the tribe of Judah, was found guilty of taking Babylonian garments, two hundred shekels of silver, and a wedge of gold. He had hidden the items in his tent. Joshua and all of Israel took Achan, his family, and his possessions to the valley of Achor. They stoned them with stones until they died. Then their bodies and possessions were burned; it was the destruction of an entire nation.

How many nations have been stopped because of their sins? Could this very thing happen in the United States at this time?

God instructed Joshua to go back to Ai because He had given the king, his people, and his land into Joshua's hand. God told Joshua that he would do to Ai and its king as he had done to Jericho. God was again on the side of the mighty men of Israel and when Joshua did as he was instructed, the army prevailed and the city of Ai was taken in the name of the Lord.

Before it could conquer Ai, the army of Israel had to remove all the sin that was in its camp. Are we sometimes stopped before we can achieve the victory God has promised us? Despite our busy lives, do we stop to reflect and consider if there is sin in our camp? If so, there is a prerequisite to gaining victory, and that is to *get rid of the sin in the camp!*

Joshua built an altar to the Lord God of Israel as Moses had instructed him to do. This altar was built with whole stones upon which no man had wielded an iron tool, as recorded in Deuteronomy 27:5-6. In the presence of the children of Israel, Joshua wrote the Law of Moses on the stones. He then read all the words of the law, the blessings and the curses.

Joshua 9:1-2 describes how the kings of the other nations gathered together to fight Israel. These were the Hittites, Amorites, Canaanites, Perizzites, *Hivites*, and Jebusites, all of whom lived on the other side of the Jordan. Let us now recall when we first discussed the Hivites. The father of Shechem, the man who defiled Jacob's daughter Dinah, was a Hivite prince. The Hivites had agreed to the Covenant of Circumcision so that their tribe could become as the Jews and could intermarry. The two sons killed the Hivites on the third day after they were circumcised, so that they would not become as their tribe. Dinah's brothers dealt deceitfully with Shechem and his father and destroyed the males of their house instead of honoring the covenant they had made with them. Now we will see how God respects covenants.

The citizens of Gibeon, a Hivite town, heard about the defeat of Jericho and Ai. They worked craftily and deceitfully and sent out men pretending to be ambassadors. They put old sacks on their donkeys, and carried old, torn wineskins. They put old, worn, and patched sandals on their feet and worn-out garments on their bodies. Their food was dry and moldy. They then presented themselves to Joshua and asked the children of Israel to make a covenant with them. The children of Israel said to them, "Perhaps you live among us, so why would we form a league with you?" They replied, "No, we only come to be your servants."

Joshua asked them, "Who are you and from where have you come?" They replied:

> We have come from a very far country. We heard of the fame of your God and what He did in Egypt, how He dealt with the kings of the Amorites who were beyond the Jordan, with Sihon, king of Hesbon, and Og, king of Bashan, which was at Ashtaroth. Therefore, the elders and inhabitants of

our country told us to take provisions with us for a long journey and to say that we were to be your servants. We would like to make a league with you. This is our bread that we took hot from our ovens on the day we departed but now look and see that it is molded and dry. These wineskins, which we filled were new, but behold now they are rent. Our garments and shoes have also become old because of the long journey.

Without seeking the counsel of the Lord, the men of Israel took some of their provisions to give to the imposters. So Joshua made peace and a covenant with the Hivites that they should live, and the rulers of the congregation swore this to them. Three days after making covenant, the Israelites heard that the Hivites were indeed their neighbors.

The children of Israel went into the Hivite cities of Gibeon, Chephirah, Beeroth, and Kirjath Jearim. They did not make war with them because the rulers of the congregation had sworn by the name of the Lord God of Israel not to do so. The congregation murmured and complained about the rulers, but they replied, "We have sworn to them by the Lord God of Israel; therefore, now we cannot touch them. Let them live lest wrath come upon us for the oath that we swore to them. Let them become hewers of wood and drawers of water, for the entire congregation, as the princes had promised them."

Joshua called all of the Hivites and said to them, "Why have you deceived us by telling us you were from a far country when you actually live very close to us? Therefore, you are cursed, and none of you shall be freed from being slaves." They answered Joshua, saying:

> We were very much afraid because your servants were very clearly told that the Lord your God commanded Moses to destroy all the inhabitants of the country that He had given to the children of Israel. [*Author's note:* They felt it would be better to be cursed than dead.] And now here we are in your hands to do with us as it pleases you.

Joshua made them hewers of wood and drawers of water for the congregation and the altar of God.

Consider the importance and, yes, the necessity of always inquiring with the Lord God before making a covenant concerning anything in your life. The children of Israel did not inquire of the Lord their God before making covenant with these Hivites. Therefore, they were bound by the words of their mouths. We now realize that because of deceit the Hivites were cut off from the Hebrews, and because of deceit they were returned to the Hebrew family.

Deuteronomy 7 explains that the children of Israel were to destroy, as if they had never existed, the nations that God delivered unto them. They were not to make any covenants with them or show them any mercy. When they failed to obey their Lord God, they set themselves up to be continually harassed by these nations for generations. As the book of Deuteronomy explains, God also told the children of Israel that he required them to do five things:

1. To fear or stand in awe of the Lord your God
2. To walk in all of His ways
3. To love Him
4. To serve Him with all your heart and soul
5. To keep His commandments and the statutes that He has established for our own good

These five things are as relevant today as they were to the Hebrew children back then.

The king of Jerusalem, Adoni-Zedek, heard about the destruction of Ai and Jericho and how the inhabitants of Gibeon had made peace with Israel. He gathered five other kings into an alliance, went to Gibeon, and waged war against the inhabitants of the city. The men of Gibeon sent a plea to Joshua at his camp at Gilgal, asking him not to forget his servants. (Although Joshua's covenant with these men was based on deception, God will honor a covenant no matter what had transpired to create the agreement.) They pleaded for Joshua to deliver them and save them from Adoni-Zedek and the other kings.

Joshua, all the men of war, and all the mighty men of valor left Gilgal and went to destroy the enemies of Gibeon. The Lord God told Joshua that he was not to fear those enemies because He would deliver them into Joshua's hand, and no man would stand before him. Joshua came upon the five kings and their armies suddenly, after marching all night from Gilgal. The Lord routed the armies before Israel and killed them in a great slaughter. As the armies fled, the Lord God cast down huge hailstones from heaven, and they died. More were killed with hailstones than were killed with the sword.

Joshua spoke to the Lord God, saying in the sight of all Israel, "Sun, stand still over Gibeon, and moon, in the valley of Aijalon." Then the sun stood and the moon stopped until the people had taken revenge upon the enemies of Gibeon, part of the nation of Hivites. There has never been a day like it, before or after, when the Lord heeded the voice of a man and defeated his enemies. Joshua became a hero and would be remembered for all time. The part of the story that is so important is that rarely do we go into enough study to know that the enemies that Joshua referred to was actually the enemies of the Hivites. We should remember that the Hivites were saved from their enemies because of the covenant they had with the men of Israel.

Now the questions come. Do we need time to stand still to defeat our enemies, or do we need to be saved? Do we need hailstones or a free pass?

After this, Joshua retreated to Gilgal with all of the men of Israel, and the five kings hid in a cave. When Joshua heard where they were hiding, he told the men of Israel, "Roll large stones against the mouth of the cave, and set men there to guard them. However, do not stay there but pursue your enemies, attack their rear guard, and do not allow them to seek refuge in their fortified cities." They attacked their enemies, and then all the men of war returned to their camp in peace.

Joshua then had the stone removed from the cave opening, and the five kings were brought to him. When they were in front of him, Joshua called all the men of Israel and said to the captains, "Put your feet on the neck of each king, and do not fear. The Lord will do the same to all your enemies against whom you fight."

Joshua and the Hebrew children fought many battles to conquer the lands God had promised them. When the lands were cleared of all their inhabitants and the land was divided, Joshua made a covenant with the people of Israel and a statute and an ordinance in the city of Shechem. He wrote the words in the book of the law of God and placed a large stone under the oak that was there by the sanctuary of the Lord. This stone was placed as a witness in case any of the Israelites ever denied their God.

Although the Hivites are not mentioned in the Bible after the covenant agreement, they were saved. However, most people do not realize exactly who was saved.

The willingness of Shechem, son of Hamor, to enter into a blood covenant created a marriage, so to speak, between Israel and the Hivites. Shechem, who was a Hivite prince, and his family were destroyed by Simeon and Levi, Dinah's brothers. By deceit they also were allowed back into relationship with Israel. They were brought back as servants, hewers of wood and drawers of water. They were not allowed into worship because of their actions. They were allowed to participate only because if there was no wood, there was no sacrifice, and if no water was available, the temple and the priests could not be ceremonially cleansed, and there would be no clean clothes to wear to the synagogue for the Sabbath worship and praise.

Some members of the modern church feel, as the Hivites did, that they are only servants. They consider themselves unworthy. However, if it were not for all of us and our different gifts, bestowed on us by our Heavenly Father, the mission of the church could not be accomplished.

CHAPTER 6

In this chapter, I would like to take some liberties and explain my quest and search for Jewish spiritual knowledge, traditions, and laws. To me, it always seemed that every step of their lives was determined by a set law. Even so, some still veer from the righteous path. Many members of the current generation, who have a new covenant with Jesus, Yashua, the Messiah, do not accept righteousness.

In an attempt to understand Jewish tradition, I have sought out the teachings of several Messianic Jews (who are part of a religious movement that combines Christian evangelism and Jewish ritual). One of the things that were brought to my attention was the use of a scapegoat to rid the Jewish people of sin. The following information can be found in the Talmud. The Talmud is a vast collection of Jewish Laws and Traditions. Webster's New World College Dictionary gives the following definition: The collections of writings constituting the Jewish civil and religious laws. It consists of two parts, the Mishna (text) and the Gamma (commentary). For Israel to be redeemed; sin had to be dealt with yearly. A part of the process of forgiveness for sin, as recorded in Leviticus 16:1-28, was for the priest to choose two goats and present them before God. The priest would then cast lots, for the goats. One would be for the Lord, and the other for the scapegoat. This has been a subject for controversy for years between the Christian world and Jewish Rabbincal Order.

The following is Judaism's rabbinical response to the question of the scapegoat. In accordance with Talmud, the accepted goat had a wool scrap, dyed red, attached to its head. The red scrap would turn white in the presence of the large crowd gathered at the Temple on the Day of Atonement. The Jewish people perceived this miraculous transformation as a heavenly sign that their sins were forgive. The foregoing information can be viewed in its entirety at Outreach Judasim.

According to Christian teaching, after a number of years, the temple was destroyed, and this sacrifice was never made again. After the death of

Jesus, the offering was never to turn white again. In other words, there was no more sacrifice that could pay for sins, for the Perfect Lamb had been given as the only sacrifice that would be needed? In accordance with Hebrews 9:27-28 NKJV: "And as it is appointed for men to die once, but after this the judgment, so Christ was offered once to bear the sins of many. To those who eagerly wait for Him, He will appear a second time, apart from sin, for salvation."

I have also studied with Zola Levitt, another Messianic Jew, and author of *A Christian Love Story*. In this small paperback book, Levitt describes the Jewish marriage ceremony and explains how it relates to Christ's return for His bride, the church. This book is enlightening and interesting. Copies can be purchased from Zola Levitt Ministries, PO Box 12268, Dallas, TX 75225; https://store.levitt.com.

CHAPTER 7

In his lust for the flesh, Shechem takes Dinah, who represents the old law; he lies with her and then realizes he is unable to have a relationship with her. The Gentile nation is just like Shechem; its members have raped the Hebrew religion. They have taken her pureness and defiled it. The only pureness that the Hebrew religion had was that given by the covenant law. Under the old law, a sacrifice had to be offered to cover sins, as stated in Hebrews 10:1-4(NKJV), it did not erase sins, as the blood of Christ does for Christians under the new covenant.

Therefore, we Gentiles lay down with the old Jewish law, thinking this is what we must have: a written set of do's and don'ts that we think we can live with although there is no covenant. Only an agreement or a covenant is equal to a relationship with God. While Gentiles have tried to take the old covenant, what they have taken has been a religion, not a relationship with God. Now we should see that there is nothing we can do in the flesh that will be totally pleasing to God. The old law did not save the Jewish nation; it could only keep them. A blood sacrifice had to be offered to cover their sins, not to erase them, as the blood of Christ does for us. Christ Jesus, our Messiah, was the perfect sacrifice; He was offered to keep us for eternity. If you want to know more about the old law, read all of chapter 4 of the book of Deuteronomy.

In the New Testament, Romans 3:5-20 tells us that the law was provided to identify sin. Until the law was given, man did not have a definition for sin.

Okay! Now the question is which is easier: to live under the condition in which we say, "I am just an old sinner, saved by grace," or to say, "I am under a covenant that provides eternal forgiveness of sin and allows me to claim the righteousness of my Lord and Savior, Jesus Christ."

Romans 3:21-31 explains from where our righteousness comes. The word righteousness merely means "in right standing with God." The righteousness of God is ours only because of what Jesus did, is doing, and will be doing, in us and through us. We cannot do enough work or learn enough to accomplish the lasting, eternal work of salvation. Chapters 27-28 of Romans clearly tells us that only through the law of faith in the Lord Jesus Christ can this be accomplished. The new covenant has been established and ratified through the blood that was shed on the cross at Calvary.

Some Gentiles say, "Get ready! He could come at any minute." All we can say is, "Ha!" God the Father will honor only His holy convocations, and those convocations are a celebration of man before God. God spoke them; therefore, they became binding. Numbers 23:19 states that "God is not a man that He should lie nor the son of man that He should repent." God's spoken words are yea and amen. He spoke the whole world into being, and He looked and saw that everything He made was good. The definition of good can be found in *Webster's* New World College Dictionary, which gives the meaning as "to be suitable for a purpose, producing favorable results, fertile, fresh, unspoiled, uncontaminated, valid, genuine, honorable, considered best . . ."

Based on what we can find in the Scriptures, God makes no mistakes. Mistakes are made when men and women, in their wisdom, think they know better than God what should be happening. Remember when the enemy said to Adam, "Surely God didn't mean you would die if you ate the fruit of any tree He had put in the garden." Adam replied, "I'm sure He didn't mean we would die." Today, agreement with the enemy produces the same fruit of the flesh, just as it did then. By "flesh," I mean the five senses that were given to us by the Heavenly Father. When any of these senses are contaminated, they, rather than the Holy Spirit, will lead and control us; we will find ourselves in sin.

Many people have forgotten the values on which our country was founded: a firm belief in a heavenly being,

God. This is the author's personal feeling but it is borne out in The American Patriot's Bible, the Word of God and the Shaping of America. In this work, I found a statement which is so true. It pointed out that we Americans had lost sight of the fact that we were blessed by God's choicest bounties of heaven. To be born in a land of freedom, to live in a nation founded as "One Nation Under God" by those who served the one, true God of the Bible, is both a tremendous privilege and a great responsibility. He was recognized as Father, Supplier, Giver of Life, Eternal God, Almighty God, King Eternal, etc. There are fifteen different names for God; these are but a few. This is also a conclusion that I came to upon doing some research in the aforementioned Bible. Judges 17:5-6 describes a man called Micah, who set up his own shrine, made an ephod (a vest worn by priests) and household idols; then he consecrated his son as a priest. In verse 6, the Scriptures explain that in those days there was no king, and the people did what was right in their own eyes.

Leviticus 20:13(NKJV) states, "If a man lies with a male as a woman, both of them have committed an abomination. They shall be put to death. Their blood shall be upon them."

Yes, I realize that we are now living under grace, but God has not changed His mind. In Genesis 1:28, He told the first created couple, male and female, to go, be fruitful and multiply, fill the earth and subdue it, to have dominion over everything that moves upon the earth. I believe that those who choose a different mind-set should not have the right to teach my children or serve in government. I neither want to associate or abide with them, as long as they choose that way of life.

Consider Sodom and Gomorrah, two cities mentioned in Genesis 19. They were destroyed by God, for their immorality, one form of which was homosexuality.

Look at America today. How far we have regressed from our roots in the Bible? Several states have now legalized this act of immorality. Can any of the same-sex married couples produce offspring? No. Shouldn't this tell us something? Can we separate ourselves from Sodom and Gomorrah because God has afforded us so much grace? Romans 6:1-14 tells that just because we are under grace, sin should not abound.

Is there any hope for sinners? Of course; all they have to do is repent and renounce sin. Believe in the Lord Jesus Christ and turn 180 degrees from sin. God will forgive and forget the sin. You will never have to mention that sin again, because God will put it away from Him. In every city, county, country, or state, there are Christians who will pray with sinners and give them direction for their lives.

The ways of a fool are right in his own eyes, but he who heeds counsel is wise, so states the book of Proverbs 17:15. The beginning of wisdom is to fear.

The things of God are still as spiritually good today as they were in the past, but it is mankind that has changed the meaning of "good." Therefore, there are still a lot of people walking around defeated, dejected, despised, without purpose or hope.

As many of Paul's writings explain, there is nothing in the work of flesh that can result in a lasting relationship with God. Many of these writings can be found in Romans 7-8. Read especially Romans 8:1(NKJV), which states, "There is therefore now no condemnation to those who are in Christ Jesus, who do not walk according to flesh but according to the Spirit." 1 Corinthians 1:18-29 says that no flesh should glory in His presence. Galatians 5:16-18 states that if we walk in the Spirit, we will no longer be under the law of sin and death. Galatians 5:22-26 explains that if we truly love and honor Christ, which means we have crucified our flesh with its desires. "To live in the Spirit" means to walk in the Spirit and that it is our desire to please our Heavenly Father.

John 6:47-66(NKJV) Jesus gave a Spirit Word that said, "The only way to have eternal life was through Him and that no one could come to Him unless it was granted to him by the Father. We cannot do this via works of the flesh; it has to be through the work of the Holy Spirit and God's Son, the Lord Jesus Christ.

1 John 2:1-17 tells us that the heirs to God's kingdom should live deeply and sincerely in Christ that the things of the world and the fleshly realm will pale in comparison to the things of God. If we walk and live this way, we will be taught the things of God, and we will have no need to be ashamed when He returns.

We should work toward the kingdom of God and righteousness and not to what mankind thinks the kingdom is. The meaning of kingdom in Webster's New World College Dictionary is "the position, rank, or power of a king." Since God is considered to be King in the Christian's life, then that place where He is in residence would be referred to as His Kingdom. So we will either have God as the king, or the flesh will be dictated to by the evil one, the father of lies, the deceiver, the devil, Satan, sitting on the throne. This is entirely our choice.

The education of the world cannot make us know the things of God. These cannot be discerned through a PhD or any degree but only through the discernment of the Holy Spirit and the study of Jewish history.

Do we know how our witness and testimony are accepted by those around us? Let us look at the woman who had an issue of blood for twelve years. This story can be found in Matthew 9:20-26, Mark 5:25-34, and Luke

8:43-48. Malachi 4:2 tells us that healing is in the wings, not the hem of the Lord's garment but the wings of His prayer shawl, i.e., the tassels, which are known as *tzitzit*. Numbers 15:37-41 states that faithful Jewish men wore these shawls, and the *tzitzit* had to be made in a special way.

The woman approached the Lord from behind because she was afraid. She was considered unclean, and everything she touched became unclean. In this case, the very opposite happened; mercy, grace, and faith became intertwined. Jesus's purity made her pure and whole. Jesus felt virtue leave Him, and he asked, "Who touched me?" Because she was afraid, she hesitated to admit she touched Him. By the Hebrew law of that day, she should have been put to death for her actions. Despite this threat, she had heard about the miracles of the Lord and that healing could be made available to her. In faith, she sought Him out, believing she would be healed, and she was.

She continued on her way and testified about her miracle. Meanwhile, people brought the sick to the Lord. Each patient was placed where they could reach out and touch his *tzitzit*. Everyone who touched Him was made whole. This can be found in Matthew 14:34-36.

Many of the ideas mentioned in this chapter are discussed in *Jewish New Testament Commentary: A Companion Volume to the Jewish New Testament* by David H. Stern. It can be ordered on CD-ROM from www.MessianicJewish. net.

If the Holy Spirit has not spoken to you and given the full meaning of these Scriptures to you, I apologize.

To God is the glory.

ADDENDUM

In 2 Corinthians 5:20, the apostle Paul states, "Therefore, we are ambassadors for Christ." So then, as the ambassadors of Christ, should we not represent Him, in every aspect, to others who do not know Him?

When you look at the way God has used various people in times past, doesn't it make you wonder, "If only I could be used by God in some similar way"? Well, we all know that God had a special need, at a special time, when He used those people to accomplish His goal. Maybe He has a special need, at this time, for each of us.

We are told by the apostle Paul that as followers of Christ, we are His ambassadors. According to the Webster's New World College Dictionary, an ambassador is "an official herald with a special mission." How does one become qualified to be an ambassador for Christ, and what does one need to do? (Please refer to the Bible verses in exhibit B to find the background for the following.)

1 We must accept the fact that God is the creator of all things, and He created men and women as members

of His family. As such, we are to obey Him. We must recognize that each person has at some time in his or her life disobeyed God, which is called sin, which separates us from God. To renew our relationship with God, we must confess that we have sinned against God and repent.

2. We then must recognize that Christ, who is the Son of God, came to this earth and died on the cross so that our sins can be forgiven. We must call on Jesus Christ to forgive us of our sins. Then He will reinstate us as members of God's family.

3. We need to ask God to fill us with His Holy Spirit and guide us to becoming effective witnesses for Christ. Then we should allow the Holy Spirit to sanctify us, which means to remove the carnal nature that causes us to want to sin against God.

4. Once God fills us with His Spirit, we will be qualified to be ambassadors for Christ.

5. As his ambassadors, we then need to find an effective means of witnessing for Christ. Following is one method that has proven to be quite effective for me.

Prepare a set of business cards for yourself. You can do this without a large expense if you have access to a computer.

1. Buy a computer program for creating business cards. Install it on your computer, and then use it to prepare your own cards. Be sure to include your name, address, phone number, and e-mail address. You also can create similar business cards for others who want to become ambassadors for Christ.

2. Procure business card stock.

3. Prepare your business card using the program directions and the format in exhibit A. The layout for the back of the card includes a space for the scriptural references for the plan of salvation. These biblical verses can be found in exhibit B. Most programs allow you to print multiple cards on one page.

4. Take a page of cards to a local photocopy center and make several copies on your card stock.

You now have a tool to use as an ambassador for Christ. Hand out the cards to people that you meet, such as neighbors, family, friends, etc. God will inspire you in the use of your cards.

This is only one cost-efficient idea. If you have the funds available, here are two other suggestions.

1 Order several copies of the pamphlet titled "Have You Heard of the Four Spiritual Laws?" This pamphlet lists the steps a person needs to achieve salvation through Jesus Christ. It is available from Campus Crusade for Christ, 375 Highway 74 South, Suite A, Peachtree, GA 30269, or by going online to www.campus crusade.org.

2. Order copies of the film called *Jesus*, which is available in DVD and VHS formats. It is available from the Jesus Film Project, PO Box 6228222, Orlando, FL 32862-8222, (800)387-4040, info@ jesusfilm.org. Exhibit C offers an example of a letter that you can use when you give or mail copies of the film to friends and relatives. These make excellent gifts for Christmas, birthdays, and anniversaries.

Be assured that if you ask God with an open heart and soul, He will direct you to the way He wants you to be an ambassador for Christ. May God richly bless you and guide you in your walk with Him.

EXHIBIT A

AMBASSADOR FOR CHRIST

SERVING GOD THE FATHER, CHRIST THE SON,
AND THE HOLY SPIRIT

[Your name]
[Your phone number]
[Your address]
[Your e-mail address]

EXHIBIT B

(1) "For all have sinned and fall short of the glory of God" (Romans 3:23).

(2) "For the wages of sin is death, but the gift of God is eternal life in Jesus Christ our Lord" (Romans 6:23).

(3) "For God so loved the world that he gave His only begotten Son, that whosoever believes in Him should not perish but have everlasting life" (John 3:16).

(4) "Jesus said to him, 'I am The Way, The Truth, and The Life. No one comes to the Father except through me' (John 14:6).

(5) "In my Father's house are many mansions, I go to prepare a place for you that where I am, there you may be also" (John 14:2).

Exhibit C

AMBASSADOR FOR CHRIST
[Your name]
[Your address]
[The date]

Dear Fellow Traveler on the Road of Life:

I am providing the attached DVD with the hope that you will take some time out of your busy schedule to view it. After you have seen it, or if you decide not to do so, please do one of the following:

- Keep the DVD to show to a relative or friend.
- Give the DVD, along with the packaging in which you received it, this letter, and its attachments, to a relative or friend.
- Use the attached blank address label and postage to mail the DVD to a relative or friend; again including this letter and the attachments.

- Use the attached postage-paid envelope to return DVD to me. If you receive the DVD without such an envelope, please contact me (see below), and I will reimburse you.

As you can see from the above, it is my desire that this DVD get into the hands of as many people as possible without you having to incur any expense. I also do not want the DVD to sit on a shelf, collecting dust.

If you would like to have additional copies of the DVD to give to others, contact me or go to www.jesusfilm.org. If you have any comments or questions, please do not hesitate to contact me. I can be reached in the following ways:

- By mail or in person: *[your name and address]*
- By e-mail: *[your e-mail address]*
- By phone: *[your phone number]*

I look forward to hearing from you. May God bless you,

[Your name]